Roots, Stems, Leaves, and Flowers

Let's Investigate Plant Parts

by Ruth Owen

Published in 2017 by Ruby Tuesday Books Ltd.

Editor: Mark J. Sachner
Designer: Emma Randall
Consultant: Judy Wearing, PhD, BEd
Production: John Lingham

Photo credits:
Alamy: 23; Getty Images: 17 (top right); Ruth Owen: 10, 17 (bottom right); Science Photo Library: 22 (right); Shutterstock: Cover, 1, 2–3, 4–5, 6–7, 8–9, 11, 12–13, 14–15, 16, 17 (top left), 18–19, 20–21, 22 (left), 24–25, 26–27, 28–29, 30–31.

Library of Congress Control Number: 2016918446

ISBN 978-1-911341-43-7

Printed and published in the United States of America

For further information including rights and permissions requests, please contact our Customer Service Department at 877-337-8577.

Contents

Words shown in **bold** in the text are explained in the glossary.

The download button shows there are free worksheets or other resources available. Go to:

www.rubytuesdaybooks.com/getstarted

What Is a Plant?

A plant is a living thing. Plants come in lots of shapes and sizes.

Sunflowers

Grass

Tall tree

Tiny daisy

Even though plants look different from each other, most have the same parts.

Flower

Leaf

Stem

Roots

Scientists think there are more than 400,000 different types of plants on Earth!

What Does a Plant Need?

A plant needs a place to grow. Most plants grow in soil.

Most plants need substances called **nutrients** to help them grow and stay healthy. Plants get nutrients from soil.

Soil

A plant needs water, sunlight, and air.

Most plants grow seeds to make new plants.

Dandelion seed

The parts of a plant all have jobs to do to help a plant live, grow, and make new plants.

Let's Talk

How do you think plants take in the water they need?

What Do Roots Do?

A plant's roots grow down into the soil.

They act like drinking straws, sucking up water and nutrients from the soil.

Some plants have many roots that spread out in the soil.

Soil

Thick roots

A large tree has long, woody roots that can be as thick as a person's leg. Thinner roots, including hairlike roots, grow from the thick roots.

Carrot plant

Some plants, such as carrot plants and dandelions, have one long, main root called a taproot.

Thinner roots grow from the taproot.

Taproot

When you eat a juicy carrot, you're eating a carrot plant's root.

Thin roots

Let's Talk

A plant's roots have another important job to do. What do you think this is?

Holding on Tight

A plant's roots hold a plant in the soil.

They keep it from falling over when the wind blows.

Tree

Roots

This tree is growing on a slope. It's also been blown sideways by the wind. The tree's thick roots still hold it in place, though.

A big plant's roots keep it from toppling over if its branches become heavy.

Dandelion

A dandelion's long taproot holds the little plant firmly in the ground.

Taproot

Thin roots

Let's Test It!

Are you stronger than a dandelion's root?

1. Find a large dandelion plant in a yard or your school playground. Ask an adult if you can pull up the plant.

2. Take hold of the plant's leaves, stems, and flowers and pull as hard as you can!

   Did you manage to pull the dandelion's root from the ground?

3. Next try digging up the root with a small shovel.

   Did you manage to dig up the taproot?

   Why do you think the dandelion needs such a long root?

(The answer is at the bottom of the page.)

Answer: Dandelions often grow in places where there is not much soil. The plant's long root grows deep underground to find water and nutrients.

Growing from Bulbs

Some plants grow from an underground part called a bulb.

Leaves and flowers grow from the bulb.

The bulb contains food that gives the plant **energy**.

Bulb

Flower

Leaf

Bud

Bulb

Roots grow from the *bulb*.

Daffodils

Crocuses

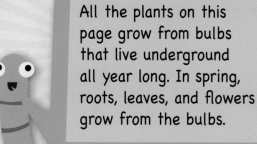

All the plants on this page grow from bulbs that live underground all year long. In spring, roots, leaves, and flowers grow from the bulbs.

Snowdrops

Tulips

All About Stems

A plant's stems are like its skeleton, or framework.

Branch

Trunk

A tree has a main stem called a trunk.

Thinner stems called branches grow from the trunk.

Bark →

A tree's trunk and branches are covered by a tough outer layer called bark.

The tree's bark protects it from rain, snow, hot sun, and being eaten by animals.

 Let's Explore!

Not all tree bark looks the same. In a yard, park, or woodland, try to find **4** different types of bark. Examine each one and record your observations in a notebook.

What color is it?

How would you describe the bark's pattern?

What does the bark feel like?

How would you describe the bark's smell?

Draw a picture of the bark you like best.

Sycamore tree

Oak tree

Beech tree

Apple tree

15

Tiny Tubes, Super Stems

A plant's stems carry water from its roots up to its leaves.

The water is carried inside tubes in the stems.

The tubes are too tiny to see with your eyes alone.

Leaf

Stem

Tubes

This picture was taken by a **microscope**. It shows the tiny tubes inside the stem of a flower.

Be a Scientist!

Test how stems work with this investigation.

Gather your equipment:
- A glass
- Water
- A stick of celery with leaves
- Red food coloring
- A teaspoon
- An adult helper

1. Pour about 2 inches (5 cm) of water into the glass. Stir two teaspoons of red food coloring into the water.

2. Ask an adult to cut 1 inch (2.5 cm) from the end of the celery stick that has no leaves.

3. Stand the cut end of the celery in the red water.

What do you think will happen? Write your ideas in a notebook.

4. Leave the celery overnight, and check the next day.

What do you observe has happened? Record the results in your notebook.

How is the celery stem like a straw?

Lots of Leaves

Plants come in many different shapes and sizes. So do their leaves.

Dandelion

Holly

Ivy

Mint plant

Cucumber plant

Geranium

Stinging nettle

Nasturtium

Oak tree

Veins

American chestnut tree

Maple tree

A leaf has thin **veins** running through it. Water is carried into the leaf along these veins.

Beech tree

Mountain ash tree

Rose

Some leaves are made up of several small leaflets on a single stalk.

Horse chestnut tree

Leaflets

Let's Explore!

Go on a leaf hunt in a yard, park, or woodland.
Collect as many different fallen leaves as you can.

Do any of the leaves match the ones in this book?

How would you describe the shapes of the leaves?
Are any of them symmetrical?

Try sorting your leaves into groups by size.
In what other ways can you sort your leaves?

Leafy Food Factories

Just like people and animals, plants need food for growth and energy.

How do plants get the food they need?

They make it inside their leaves!

A plant's leaves make food with the help of a green substance called **chlorophyll**. It's chlorophyll that gives plants their green color.

How Do Leaves Make Food?

Sunlight

Water travels from a plant's roots up into its leaves.

The leaves take in **carbon dioxide** gas from the air.

Inside its leaves, a plant uses sunlight to turn water and carbon dioxide into food for energy.

This process is called **photosynthesis**.

We All Need Leaves

To make food, a leaf takes in carbon dioxide gas through tiny holes called stomata.

Clover leaf

Stomata

A leaf has thousands of stomata.
They look like tiny mouths.
Stomata can only be seen with
a powerful microscope.

As it makes food, a leaf also produces **oxygen** gas.

It releases this gas into the air through its stomata.

Gunnera plant leaf

People and animals need oxygen to breathe.

Whether a leaf is tiny or enormous, it is making the oxygen we need to live.

Giant water lily plant leaf

Autumn Leaves

In autumn, the leaves of some trees change color and drop. Why?

During winter, a tree's leaves cannot get enough sunlight and water to make food.

Autumn

Winter

So to save energy, a tree drops its leaves and rests.

Spring

Summer

In spring, the tree grows new leaves.

Let's Talk

Why do you think a tree's leaves change color before they drop?

(The answer is at the bottom of the page.)

Trees that drop their leaves in autumn are called deciduous trees.

Answer: Leaves are green because they contain green chlorophyll. Leaves make this substance inside themselves. Once a leaf stops making food, it also stops making chlorophyll. The leaf's green color starts to fade. Then its other colors, which are normally hidden by green, show through.

25

Evergreen Trees

Some trees do not drop all their leaves in autumn. They are called evergreen trees.

Evergreen trees drop and regrow a small number of leaves all year long.

That's why these trees always look green.

Evergreen tree

Scots pine needles

Many evergreen trees have thin leaves that look like needles. The needle-like leaves make food for the tree all year round.

Each needle is a leaf!

An evergreen pine tree

A deciduous oak tree

Check It Out!

Compare the two trees in these winter pictures.

- *How are the trees similar?*

- *How are they different?*

All About Flowers

Most types of plants, including some trees, grow flowers.

Bud

A flower bud grows from a stem or twig.

The bud opens, and the flower's petals unfold.

Petals

Sunflower

Cherry tree blossoms

Primroses

Pansies

Flowers and their petals come in many different sizes, shapes, and colors. Flowers that grow on trees are known as blossoms.

Buttercup

Poppy

Horse chestnut tree blossoms

Flowers for Seeds

A plant's seeds form inside its flowers. Once a flower dies, its seeds are ready to fall to the ground.

A sunflower's seeds grow in the center of the flower.

Let's Draw It!

Draw a sunflower and label it.

- Petal
- Stem
- Leaf
- Flower
- Roots
- Seeds

A seed contains all the material needed to grow a new plant.

A poppy's seeds form inside a seedpod.

A seedpod growing

Poppy seedpod

Poppy seeds

The seedpod dries and splits open.

Then the tiny, black seeds scatter.

Glossary

carbon dioxide
(KAR-buhn dye-OK-side)
A gas in the air that plants use to make food. When people and animals breathe out, they release this gas into the air.

chlorophyll (KLOR-uh-fil)
A substance that gives plants their green color.

energy (EN-ur-jee)
The power needed by all living things to grow and live.

microscope (MYE-kruh-skope)
A piece of equipment used for seeing things that are too small to see with your eyes alone.

nutrient (NOO-tree-uhnt)
A substance that a living thing needs to grow and be healthy.

oxygen (OK-suh-juhn)
An invisible gas in the air that living things need to breathe.

photosynthesis
(FOH-toh SIN-thuh-siss)
The making of food by plants using water, carbon dioxide, and sunlight.

veins (VAYNZ)
Thin tubes that carry water through a plant's leaves. You have veins, too. They carry blood around your body.

Index